All rights reserved. Copyright 1990
by San Jose Historical Museum Association
ISBN 0-914139-09-6

Printed in USA by
The Rosicrucian Press
76 Notre Dame Avenue
San Jose, CA 95113

Limited edition 1990
Reprinted by the San Jose Historical Museum Association

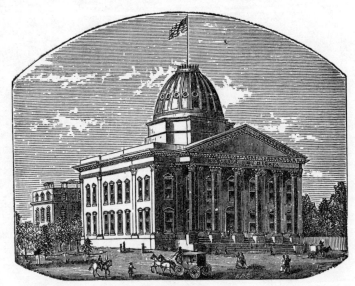

Court House.

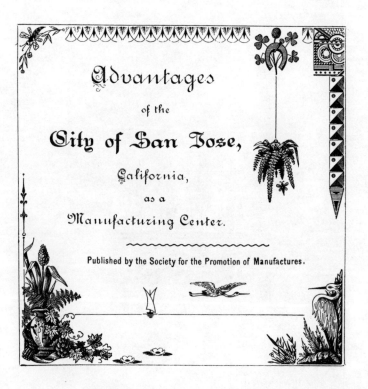

Advantages

of the

City of San Jose,

California,

as a

Manufacturing Center.

Published by the Society for the Promotion of Manufactures.

CORRECTIONS.

PAGE 14.--The statement in regard to "Frosts" is correct as to certain localities in the foot hills adjoining the valley, but in the valley proper, geraniums and fuchsias have to be protected for about two months in Winter.

PAGE 21.--First line read, "Living is in many respects," etc.

PAGE 39.--Eleventh line from top read, "Of as good a class and at as low rates as in the East."

PAGE 43.—Add to the Executive Committee, F. Field and R. F. Peckham.

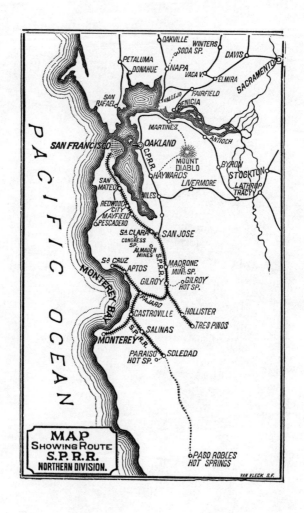

ADVANTAGES  CITY OF SAN JOSE

— AS A —

MANUFACTURING CENTER.

If it were the purpose of this pamphlet to add to existing publications describing the wondrous fertility of this valley, its unparalleled climate and marvelous beauty, such end could not better be attained than by quoting the words of the illustrious traveler and conscientious writer, Bayard Taylor, who classed it with the vale of Damascus and the valley of Mexico, and said that in scenery and soil it excelled anything he had ever seen. The following words of Henry Ward Beecher are equally clear:

" The fame of your valley has come over the plains and mountains and assailed our

ears, until, with the description of scenery,
of mountains, of mines, of trees, of shrubs,
of farms, gardens and harvests, of people
and prospects, I will not say that we are
wearied, but will say that we were somewhat
stunned, and it gave the belief that if nothing
else excelled in California, the art of ex-
aggeration was rife; and yet, having but
come as an arrow through the air, and without time to fill in my mind what I saw upon
the surface, teaches me a lesson of estima-
tion of the truth, and I will say with her of
old, ' the half has not been told me.'   This
goodly land which, furtherest from the East,
seems to have been the last work that God
had in hand, and He furnished it to suit the
home of man the best."

Scores of similar paragraphs from the
tongues and pens of other men of world-
wide fame might be reproduced were it
needful. The fact is that the fame of the
valley, as a home for the agriculturist, the
horticulturist, the pomologist, the profes-

sional man, the tradesman and the man who has retired from active life to spend his declining years where the most comfort can be obtained, is sufficiently well known, and immigration from these classes is pouring in upon us as rapidly as is compatible with healthful growth. There is one thing that we need to extend our commerce, and that is manufacturing industries.

The character of our population is here indicated: First were the natives of the soil; then the missionaries and adventurers; then the cattlemen and the agriculturists. The latter have remained, and their sons, and their sons' sons are with us still. To their ranks have been added the families of the cattlemen, and the miners who have amassed fortunes in this and neighboring States and Territories, and who have come here to enjoy the advantages of climate, schools, and all that makes life worth the living, for which Santa Clara county is preeminent. To these, also, must be added a heavy and constantly increasing immigration from the Eastern States, but the latter, almost without exception, charmed with the beauties of California suburban life, at once find congenial and remunerative employment in the culture of fruit. It must here be remarked that the growing of cereals has had its day in this valley, and that the agriculturist who drove out the breeder of long-horned cattle and proclaimed wheat as King, is himself, with gigantic strides, making room for the horticulturist and the pomologist, or learning their arts. Unlike the stock-raiser, however, he goes not repiningly, for he has satisfied himself beyond the shadow of a doubt that there is a bonanza in his broad acres such as was never dreamed of on the Comstock. With these statements, it will be readily understood that our people are strangers, so far as practical knowledge is concerned, to the manufacturing industries of the East, though they are fully alive to their importance and have carefully studied

San Jose, Looking North, from Electric Light Tower.

the conditions requisite to their inception and successful conduct. There is money here in abundance, and it will be freely furnished to all who can establish their integrity and capability to found and maintain a manufacturing industry; and it is for the purpose of indicating our resources that "the Society for Promotion of Manufactures in San Jose" has caused this little book to be published.

What are its resources? The county is about 52 miles in length, with an average width of 34 miles. It contains an area of 1,759 square miles, or 1,125,760 acres, of which a little less than one-half is valley, and the remainder grassy hills or timbered mountains. While there exists a wide variety of soil, and some locations are especially favored for tropical or semi-tropical fruits, there can scarcely be said to be any "best land" or choice location. It is all best. The requirements, to the highest degree of perfection, for different varieties

of fruit and vines being as diverse as the
soils. There is not an acre of the valley or
hill land, and scarcely one of the mountain
sides upon which many varieties of fruit or
vine may not be profitably grown. The
profits are immense. Four hundred dollars
per acre from an orchard or vineyard of
matured trees or vines is not an infrequent
yield. The local fruit canneries and dryers
have never been able to supply the demand
made upon them. Their market is the
world, and there is not the slightest prospect
of over-production. Should prices for fruit
diminish to one-fourth of what they have
been since the canneries were established
five acres of land would still maintain an
ordinary family in comfort, and ten acres
keep them in affluence. The valley is capa-
ble of supporting an immense population on
its land alone. It is now largely divided up
into homesteads of the size indicated, and
the work goes on. Orchards and vineyards
are being multiplied as rapidly as nurseries

have thus far been able to supply the stock. The present population is about 40,000. The assessed valuation for 1883 in round numbers is 30,000,000.

San Jose is the capital of Santa Clara County. It is located in about the geographical center of the valley, 50 miles from San Francisco, and six miles from an arm of San Francisco Bay, the terminus of which is the village of Alviso, the latter place being the shipping port for most of the goods transferred to or from the metropolis by water.

San Jose has at present, including its suburbs, a population of about 16,000, and is the fourth city in the State. Surrounded as she is, in the midst of a country of remarkable fertility, and with a climate unsurpassed in healthfulness and salubrity, she has before her a future second to none. The city proper covers an area of about a mile and a half square, and lies between the Coyote and Guadalupe rivers, though the suburbs, which are accessible by street cars,

reach well out on the east, and on the west
along the famous " Alameda" to the village
of Santa Clara, three miles distant.

San Jose has more than forty miles of
level and graded streets, for the most part
lined with shade and ornamental trees.
Her water supply is abundant and comes
from two sources: artesian wells, and from
mountain streams, the latter being tapped
high up in the hills and the water brought
to the city in pipes in quantities sufficient
for all present and future necessities. The
city is lighted by electricity, the lamps being
placed on a high tower and masts, and the
system gives great satisfaction, lighting up
the outskirts which in many towns are un-
provided for. There is also a gas company
which furnishes an excellent article at reasonable rates. The Fire Department is a
mixed one—paid and volunteer. It is ex-
cellently manned and equipped. Four daily
papers, and three weeklies are sustained.
All the religious denominations are repre-

Bank of San Jose Building.

sented, and there are twelve church edifices, many of them handsome and commodious. Public buildings are superior; the Court House is considered a model of architecture, and was erected at a cost of $200,000; the private residences as a class are also tasteful and substantial. There are three banks in successful operation. The town supports one first-class theater and a number of public halls. There are several public squares in the center of town; and, a few miles out over a delightful road, the city maintains a park of 400 acres, on which there are mineral springs, and which is a very popular resort. In the matter of schools and colleges this city is pre-eminent in this and adjacent States. The Normal School is located here and has elegant buildings and grounds. There are Catholic and Protestant colleges for both young ladies and young gentlemen, which have good buildings and are well equipped. Our public schools occupy five two-story buildings, conveniently located, and include a fine night school. The schools are systematically graded and an excellent corps of teachers maintained. There is also a Commercial College and a number of excellent academies and boarding schools under the management of private individuals. The city maintains an excellent Free Library and Reading Room, and we have the usual telegraph and telephone facilities.

The situation of the city between two streams provides unexcelled facilities for natural drainage and a perfect system of sewerage has been adopted. Within the year a main sewer of a most substantial character has been constructed at a cost of over $100,000. Its terminus is the tide water at Alviso, which is 80 feet below the level of San Jose. More than two miles of it is of substantial masonry, oval shaped, and its dimension three by four and a half feet. It will endure for ages, and its capacity will be ample when the city shall have increased a hundred fold. The city is entirely free from debt of any character, and the charter provides that no expense shall be incurred unless there is money in the Treasury to meet it.

The assessed value of city property for the current year is, in round numbers, $10,000,000. The rate of taxation for all purposes is limited by the charter to $1.00 on the $100.

The Summer season here practically extends from May to December, though in some years there are showers in October and generally rains enough in November to enable the farmers to plow. Between the months named, as a rule, the only winds are the ocean breezes, which by the time they reach us are tempered to the degree sufficient to render the season delightful. In midsummer, when the thermometer marks ninety degrees, it is an event of note. Neither do these figures mean what they do in the Eastern cities, the atmosphere being less humid here, the sense of suffocation is unknown. This is attested

by the absence of sun-stroke so common in
New York and elsewhere. The remainder
of the year the winds are from the south,
and they also are shorn of their force by a
range of mountains. From December to May
is called the rainy season, but it must not be
inferred that the rains are continuous. Ordinarily the rains come in showers, succeeded
by days and sometimes weeks of bright
sunshiny weather, and the roads, freed from
dust, are in their best condition. There are
however occasional Winters when the con-
trary is the rule. No snow falls in the
valley, and the frosts are not severe enough
to harm the most tender plants. Geraniums,
fuchsias, and many other shrubs, which, in
the East must be carefully housed, here
grow luxuriantly out of doors. Our Winters
almost correspond to Spring in the Eastern
States. The rains start the vegetation,
grass springs into life, and the hills put on
their mantle of green. It is the busy time
for the agriculturist.

Theodore Lenzen,

Architect,

Opposite Masonic Temple,
San Jose, Cal.

We give here the result of careful ther-
mometrical observations for one year, which
will give, accurately, the average tempera-
ture of our city.

MONTH	Deg. 6 A. M.	Deg. 12:30 P. M	Deg. 6 P. M
June,..............	52:40	77:03	60:40
July,............ ...	55:32	81:87	64:84
August, ...	53:16	83:17	64:84
September,........	55:63	79:68	65:16
October,...........	46:38	74:68	63:06
November,........	34:40	56:77	52:30
Dcember,..........	36:61	53:68	45:26
January, ...	36:68	54:42	48:00
February,.........	38:93	58:32	48:61
March,.	39:99	62:58	51:29
April,.............	50:37	69:23	54:00
May,............. ...	48:26	69:90	54:97

It is an accepted fact that manufacturing
interests do not usually center in large cities,
as is illustrated in the cases of Cambridge,
Worcester, Gloversville and many others
that might be named. Other things being
equal, suburban towns are preferred. The
reasons are obvious. In large cities suitable
sites are difficult to obtain, and sometimes in-
accessible. Rent and taxes are oppressive,
and the hazard of fire so great as to make insurance almost impracticable. The class of labor

obtainable is not such, as a rule, as that upon
which those who have large interests at
stake care to depend. They must be freed
from the communistic spirit incited by dema-
gogues and fostered by unhappy surround-
ings which lead not only to strikes, entailing
suffering on employes and loss to employer,
but destroy the mutual sympathy and respect
between master and man so necessary to the
comfort and welfare of each, and to the best
practical results. It is requisite, however,
that a location be selected accessible to lines
of transportation, where labor may be obtained and where freight-rates are satisfactory,
and where fuel and water are to be had at
reasonable prices.

We have said that San Jose is near the
center of the valley. It is also very near
the geographical as well as the commercial
center of the State, and is on the direct line
of all of the great transcontinental railroads.
Passengers and freight by the Southern
Pacific route will all pass through here, and

the same by the Central Pacific, reach this city as quickly as they do San Francisco. In other words freights by the Southern route, in either direction are a little cheaper than to or from San Francisco, while by the Central Pacific they are identically the same.

Though in a valley, San Jose is not hemmed in by mountains. The Southern Pacific railroad runs out to the South on nearly a dead level, through a natural pass through the counties of San Benito and Monterey, and in a few weeks the last spike will be driven connecting it with the road from the South, and thus avoiding a slight detour now necessary. From here north ward this road follows the western line of San Francisco Bay. The Central Pacific runs daily trains on the east side of the bay and out through the Livermore pass to Stockton, Sacramento, and points further on, making also connections with San Francisco. Besides these roads, the South Pacific Coast road (Narrow Gauge) connects us with Santa Cruz, on the ocean beach, thirty miles southwest, and following the easterly shore of the bay, unites us to San Francisco on the northeast. Withal there is the bay itself on which competition is always free. It will be seen at a glance that there is no danger of oppressive freights.

Sites suitable for manufacturing purposes can be procured at nominal figures directly upon the line of either of these roads, so that manufactured products can be loaded from the factory upon the car and shipped without change by either the Central Pacific or Southern routes to the East, and to most of the Pacific Coast States and Territories, and to all of them as soon as a slight gap is spanned on the California and Oregon Railroad, and connection is made with the Northern Pacific Railroad. In the mean time the Pacific Ocean is at our service as a means of connecting us with Oregon and the adjacent Territories, and the service of ocean steamers and sailing vessels is ample.

San Jose, Looking North-East, from Electric Light Tower.

The Narrow Gauge Railroad taps the Coast Range mountains, thirteen miles distant, containing unlimited forests, supplying lumber and fuel, tanbark and quarries of lime and stone. Four-foot wood is laid down here at about five dollars a cord, while coal is but a trifle higher than in San Francisco. Water is abundant and pure, and can be had at a small expense.

The very best class of labor can be obtained at very reasonable rates, a little higher prices of course prevailing where extra skill is required, and for foremen and those in charge of departments. The local fruit canneries, which run only about five months in the year, employ between 1,000 and 1,200 persons, mostly women and girls. These are the wives and daughters of our good citizens, reputable and honored. Most of them are in comfortable circumstances and own their own homes. This class of labor ranges at from 50 cents to $1.25 per day, averaging, perhaps, $1. It is most satisfac-

tory to employers. This class of labor can
be supplied without limit, if constant work is
assured. It is an accepted fact that in this
equable climate, with no extremes of heat
and cold and no depressing fogs, in a
given number of hours, operatives will perform from twenty to twenty-five per cent
more labor with less fatigue than in Eastern
cities, or in less favored localities on this
coast. This is the unvarying testimony of
hundreds of skilled mechanics from New
York, Chicago, St. Louis, and other centers.

As a place of residence, San Jose presents
superior attractions to employers and employes. Comfortable homes can be secured
at very low rates reasonably near the business center, and in the suburbs accessible
by street cars, at prices within the reach of
all. Those who prefer to rent can obtain
good houses of five and six rooms, with
garden and other conveniences, at prices
ranging from $8 to $15 per month. Those
who are conversant with the facts, know

that living here is in all respects cheaper than in most Eastern cities or towns.

Ninety-five per cent of all the goods found in our hardware, dry goods and general furnishing goods stores are manufactured in the older States and in Europe, while it is confidently believed that fully seventy-five per cent, if not more, of such goods can be made as well and more cheaply here. We have in abundance the raw material which enters into most of these goods. Much of this material, such as wool, hides, mohair and many other articles, is sent East, over three thousand miles of railroad at high rates of freight, is manufactured and returned to us at still higher rates of freight, to which must be added the profits of the middlemen. It is a plain proposition that if these goods can be manufactured as cheaply in San Jose, a large margin would be saved which, if fairly divided between manufacturer and consumer, would inure to the benefit of all. It is not claimed that *all* goods

can be manufactured here as cheaply
as in the East, but that many can, and some
even at lower figures. It is also maintained
that in many cases where the cost of manufacture in San Jose is, say ten per cent higher
than in the East, the manufacturer would
here realize twenty per cent better prices.

Believing, as has been stated, that San
Jose is an especially desirable location
for many branches of manufacture that are
not now carried on here, a meeting of
citizens was called and committees were ap-
pointed to collect information upon this
subject and to present the same to the public, and especially to place facts before manufacturers and skilled workmen in the older
States and in Europe, who may desire a new
field of enterprise. Our population and
wealth is increasing in geometrical progres-
sion. In 1870 we numbered 560,247, and
at the last census, in 1880, we had grown to
864,686, an increase of more than fifty-four
per cent. The census of 1890 will undoubt-

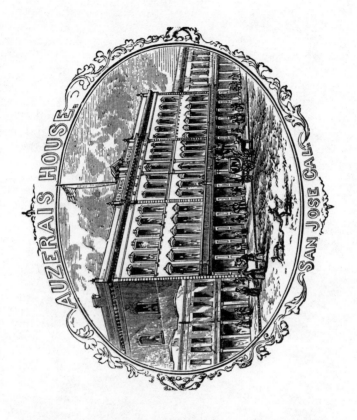

E. DELLWIG, Proprietor.

European and American plans.

edly show a greatly increased per centage of gain. Of adjacent States and Territories, which receive their supplies through San Francisco, Nevada has a population of 62,-265; Oregon a population of 174,767; Arizona a population of 40,441; Idaho a population of 32,611; New Mexico a population of 119,565; Washington Territory a population of 75,120; Utah a population of 143,906. We also supply Montana and Wyoming with many articles, and would with more if we had the factories. The material resources of this vast region have only begun to be developed, and give magnificent promise for the future. When we add to these the growing trade with Mexico and the South American ports, Australia, New Zealand, British Columbia, the South Sea Islands, China and Japan, the grand depot for which must be San Francisco Bay and its vicinity, the importance of San Jose as a manufacturing center can not well be over-estimated.

For the States and Territories already named, and to the populous nations of China, Japan, and all the South American and Mexican ports, as well as Australia, New Zealand and the South Sea Islands, San Francisco must ever be the grand commercial center.   She has been aptly described as the half-way house of the world, and to her more than half the civilized world does and ever must, in some manner, pay tribute. At present this tribute, in the main, consists of the handling of freight between car and ship.   Chicago and other manufacturing centers ship not only to California and the other Pacific States and Territories, but to Mexico and the foreign countries named, their wagons, agricultural implements, woolen goods and the very candles that our miners use in the tunnels from whence our gold and silver is dug.   While we, by way of compensation, in very many cases furnish them the raw material, paying the freight charges both ways, as well as the charges of middlemen. This can not, in the nature of things, continue, and those who first utilize the natural advantages offered, will reap abundant harvests. The Pacific Coast States and Territories are all being very rapidly settled, and their markets for articles which can be profitably manufactured in San Jose are constantly and rapidly increasing.

In this little city of San Jose more than $100,000 worth of carpets are sold annually, all the material for which are raised here and are shipped East. Outside of rag carpet, nothing in this line is manufactured upon the Pacific Coast.

We ship East annually over 200,000 pounds of mohair which is manufactured in Pennsylvania and Connecticut and returned to us in plushes and dress goods. Large quantities of the manufactured goods are used on this coast. A manufactory here would save the cost of transportation both ways and profits of middlemen. It is well known that the manufacturers of these goods in Pennsylvania and in Connecticut have amassed immense fortunes very rapidly. The Eastern shipments represent but a moiety of the mohair clip that would be available, as, for want of a local manufactory, a large number of the pelts are made into buggy robes, floor rugs, gloves, etc., of which there are three flourishing factories in San Jose whose market is even wider than has been indicated; a very small percentage of the gloves being required on the Pacific Coast, where such things are seldom worn for warmth, but only in driving or a matter of dress.

In the city of San Jose hats and caps are sold to the value of $50,000 annually, and there is on the entire coast but one establishment where they are made, and that is a small concern in San Francisco, recently established, which is proving a gratifying success.

While there are several furniture factories on the coast, all doing well, there is no

First Ward School.

place where chairs are made. This would be from the start a paying enterprise, and would not require more than $5,000 capital.

But a small proportion of the boots and shoes consumed on the Pacific Coast are manufactured this side of the Rocky Mountains, though sending abroad immense quantities of leather to be returned as manufactured goods.

The same may be said of the large quantity of candles used in the mines and for domestic uses. San Francisco Bay is the headquarters for the whaling fleets. Tallow is one of our leading productions and petroleum in unlimited quantities has been found within this county.

A line of manufactures that is almost untouched is that of farm wagons and agricultural implements. For the season of 1882 a single San Jose firm, with a hardware department attached, brought from the East and sold to its customers two car loads of wagons, one hundred wheel-barrows, one car load of harrows, one car load of mowers, and one of harvester, mowers and binders. A dozen other firms could show about the same amount of business. For these goods the market is practically unlimited, and Chicago, South Bend, and other well known cities are to-day sending their goods to all the points we have named, and are building up an immense trade in Mexico. Another reason why this industry will be especially lucrative is that the climate and soils of the Pacific Coast are so different from those in the East that the implements made there do not, as a rule, give satisfaction here, and must be frequently altered to be utilized, or if used as they come, they do not do the work satisfactorily. Eastern made wagons, carriages, separators, fanning mills, and other machinery principally composed of wood, are not adapted to our long Summer season, and check and shrink unduly.

Our farmers do not farm like Eastern farmers and demand different implements.

This opens up a fine field for inventive genius, valuable suggestions being often furnished by the granger patron, who knows exactly what he requires. The constantly increasing tendency to small farms and high cultivation renders this a most inviting field. It is true that, of hardwood, suitable for the best work, there is a scarcity on this coast; but the freight on this in the plank is so small compared with that on manufactured articles that this cuts scarcely any figure.

There is no better location in the United States for a cotton mill. There is now but one in the State, and the consumption in the territory indicated is of course enormous. There is now considerable cotton raised in the State, and with the establishment of mills the growing of this crop will receive increased attention. Considerable cotton is grown in Mexico, and quite a quantity is brought here from Tahiti and the South Sea Islands. Texas, however, which produces one-sixth of the cotton crop of the United

States, would be depended on for the present
to furnish the bulk of the raw material, but
as that State is but half-way east the differ-
ence in freight on raw and manufactured
goods, in favor of the former, will leave a
handsome margin to the manufacturer.

There is already well under way in San
Jose a manufactory of dress silks which
turns out a superior quality of goods, which
find a ready sale at remunerative prices.
Its proprietor, whose father before him was a
silk manufacturer in Lyons, France, declares
that this is the most favorable country in
the world for the cultivation of the mulberry
and the propagation of the silk worm, and
is confident that he is but the pioneer in an
industry that shall make us both wealthy
and famous.

The manufacture of perfumes, dyes, etc.,
might be profitably entered into here. We
are nearer to the South Sea Islands than
New York, and as close to the tropics,
whence come the barks and plants mostly re-

California Theater,

Second Street,

San Jose, California.

~~~~~~~~~~~~~~~~~~~~~~

Seats 1500 People.

All Modern Improvements.

~~~~~~~~~~~~~~~~~~~

Hayes & Downer,

Proprietors.

quired, and New York of scented goods alone produces annually $1,094,700 worth.

California produces annually from 45,-000,000 to 50,000,000 pounds of wool. Of this about three-fourths is shipped East, and returns to us again in blankets, cloths and ready-made clothing. The remainder is consumed by our own mills. We have already one woolen mill in San Jose, the fame of whose products is as well known East as on this coast, and which has always been very profitable to the stockholders. There is room for several more.

There is a good opening for the manufacture of ready-made clothing, all kinds of knit underwear, wool, hosiery, all kinds of knit shawls, sacks, cardigan jackets, woven woolen shawls, blankets, flannels, cassimeres and cloakings. Some of these things are now manufactured in California, but not nearly enough to supply the demand.

Fine shirts, overalls, ladies' and gents'

linen collars, can also be made at a good profit, as can trunks and valises.

Our most reliable dry goods men and clothiers say that the foregoing articles comprise one-fourth of the goods they sell, and declare that they can be profitably manufactured in San Jose.

The business of paper making is also carried on profitably to a limited extent, and there is no reason why the Pacific Coast consumption should not be fully met. The manufacture of straw and manilla paper and the manufacture of manilla bags has proved lucrative in this vicinity, and it is believed that the manufacture of news, if not letter paper, would be equally so.

The manufacture of salt might be entered into with great profit. No better location for "beds" can be found than the Alviso marshes, and none better than San Jose for the mill, as this is the center for a large dairying interest, and is a most favorable shipping point for any portion of the coast trade. The great bulk of the salt used on this coast is as yet shipped from the East, there being but one salt mill on the coast and that in San Francisco.

The manufacture of cigars is carried on in a small way, but energetic men will yet find abundant room. The putting up of smoking and chewing tobacco and the man-facture of cigarettes is in San Jose a virgin field.

Linen and hempen fabrics of all kinds could be manufactured here. Experience has abundantly proved that flax grows lux-uriantly, and the only reason it is not more extensively cultivated is that there are no factories to utilize the fiber. That which is grown is produced only for the seed, the stalk being thrown away.

Sugar is at present controlled by one company whose refineries are located in San Francisco. They levy immense tributes on our fruit industry and upon the people, and are amassing fortunes almost daily; but a vast proportion of this valley, and of the State, grows sugar beets and sorghum to perfection, and men of energy will soon compel the company referred to to divide its profits with them.

Rope of various kinds is manufactured to some extent on the coast, but the supply is not equal to the demand. Beside the ordinary uses to which it is put, vast quantities are required in this and adjoining counties for bailing hay, straw, hops, etc.

Baskets and willow ware may be manufactured with profit at a small outlay of capital. The osier willow grows indigenously along our streams.

Wooden ware of all kinds could be made here. The only manufactures in this line at present are boxes and washboards. Both of these industries are very prosperous.

The same may be said of brushes and brooms.

There is an immense field at a small outlay for the manufacture of bags for grain,

Second Ward School.

wool, flour, etc., and for tents and awnings. When it is understood that the entire grain crop of the coast must be sacked before it is moved, some idea may be had of the consumption of bags on the Pacific slope.

The manufacture of belting and hose would also pay. The market is a 'wide one; the raw product of the very best quality right in our midst.

The manufacture of wire work could be profitably engaged in.

In the foregoing catalogue, which might be indefinitely extended, manufactories already represented in San Jose have, almost without exception, been avoided and will be noticed separately.

A few of the manufacturing enterprises successfully conducted here and but partially supplying the demand, is subjoined:

The San Jose Woolen Mills has a capital invested of $250,000, and employs nearly 200 persons. It has only stopped running once in four years, and then only for a few

weeks; and yet the city of San Jose purchased last year $10,000 worth of woolen
goods from the Oakland Mills, to say nothing of Eastern goods imported. The goods
manufactured here consist of a superior
quality of blankets and cassimeres.

There are two grist mills that manufacture
a superior quality of flour for home use,
and an ordinary brand for the China trade.

Three glove factories employ in the ag-
gregate about 200 persons. They use
principally Angora goat skins, and find a
market all over the world.

There are four fruit canning companies
which are enlarging their capacities yearly.
Their output, so far, is limited only by the
supply of fruit, as their products are usually
sold before the packing season is completed.

There are two foundries and machine
shops, employing some eighty men.

There are three lumber yards and three
planing mills.

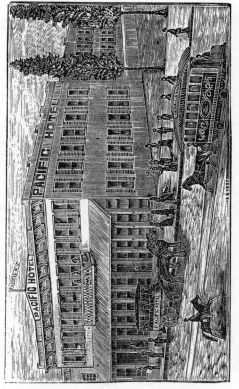

Pacific Hotel, 373 and 375 Market Street. CHAS. M. SCHIELE, Proprietor.

We have one highly successful furniture factory which employs thirty men and is driven to its full capacity.

There are ten wagon and carriage shops, mainly employed in custom work and repairing.

There are two box factories, at each of which washboards are also made.

There are five cigar factories, mostly small; four manufacturers of tin and sheet iron ware and well pipe, five marble, granite and sandstone working establishments; two manufacturers of clothing, which might perhaps be more properly classed as merchant tailors.

There is one manufactory of wind-mills, one of leather, one of paint, a small one of soap. There is also a broom factory and a coffee and spice mill.

Having given a partial list of the manufactures which it is believed could be profitably carried on here, we will now sum up the advantages therefor in San Jose.

San Jose is near the geographical center of the State of California.

San Jose is on the line, and near the terminus, of the trans-continental railroads and their feeders, by means of which such supplies of raw materials as are not produced in our midst can be and are cheaply laid down at the very doors of manufacturing establishments located within the city limits.

Besides these railroads, San Jose is adjacent to an arm of the San Francisco Bay, navigable for all classes of vessels.

We communicate daily by three lines of railroads with the 300,000 inhabitants of San Francisco who are using manufactured articles, mostly imported from abroad at great cost, which very cost is an actual protective tariff in favor of home manufacturers, and from the nature of the case this advantage will exist for many years, if not forever.

We are, by means of railroads, by bay, river and ocean navigation, in a position to receive from and distribute to all parts of

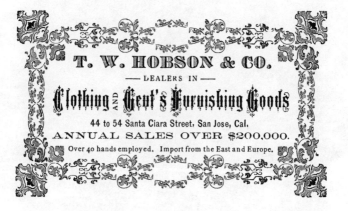

the State, the Pacific Coast, Mexico, Australia and the world at large. We offer unlimited choice of locations and ample room for manufacturing enterprises directly upon railroad trunk lines.

San Jose is surrounded with richer, more varied and more exhaustless natural resources than any other city in the world.

The class of labor to be had is superior, and factory operatives can be had of a better class and at lower rates than in the Eastern States, from the fact that a young population has just grown up, who have had, up to this time, but little chance of employment.

We enjoy a climate the most favorable for human exertion, enabling the operative to perform with ease from 25 to 30 per cent more labor in a given time than in other localities. There are no extremes of heat and cold. Snow never falls. No acclimating process is required for immigrants or persons moving from the East hither.

Employers and laborers may provide for themselves cheap and pleasant homes.

The mortality of this city is the lowest of any city in the world of its size.

There is absolutely no ague or other malarial disease.

The cost of living and rents are as low, if not lower, than can be found in nine-tenths of the cities of similar size in the United States.

The educational facilities enjoyed by this community are far in advance of other portions of the Pacific Coast and fully up to the highest standard known in the United States.

Building materials are cheap. The best lumber can be had at about $20 per thousand feet; bricks, $7 to $10 per thousand, and other articles in proportion; of special items we mention that fire-bricks of the best quality (imported) are cheaper by far than on the Atlantic Coast.

Fuel (coal) for manufacturing purposes, of the best quality, can be had by the cargo at reasonable rates.   Petroleum, for fuel, can be had still cheaper.

The city supply of water is ample for all purposes, cheap and lasting; but those requiring water of unusual purity for manufacturing can obtain artesian water in unfailing supplies, at prices heretofore indicated, which are less by from three to ten fold than in other portions of the State.

Vast as is the territory which comprises our natural markets, the Pacific Coast States and Territories, the South Sea and British Islands and South American ports and Mexico, these countries are yet in the infancy of their development and will continue to grow, and their wants and necessities to multiply till they shall have increased an hundred fold.   Besides these are the teeming millions of China and Japan, with whom we have a large and rapidly increasing commerce, which, by reason of our contiguity, can not be wrested from us by competition.

City taxes are limited to a maximum rate

of one cent on the $100. The city has no
debt and has a balance in her treasury.
County five per cent bonds, payable in five
years, are sought for at 2½ per cent premium.

An effort will be made to induce the next
Legislature to exempt all new manufacturing
enterprises from taxation for a term of years.

There are many other points of advantage as to supplies and markets, situated as
we are within a short time and distance from
the Eastern Continent, which can not be
stated in detail within the limits of this
pamphlet, but which will be apparent to all
who are disposed to give the subject attention.

In conclusion, this Society would repeat
the statement and proposition made at the
beginning of this work, to-wit: That we
have here a large amount of money seeking
investment, and that all necessary financial
aid will be extended to any person who
can demonstrate his capability of conducting
successfully any manufacturing enterprise

SAN JOSE, LOOKING EAST, FROM ELECTRIC LIGHT TOWER.
Mt. Hamilton in the Distance.

which will utilize any of the many valuable resources we have enumerated. To this end we cordially invite a personal inspection and investigation of the matters herein set forth, confidently believing that if the inquirer means business he will not hesitate about availing himself of the advantages herein offered.

We give here a list of the officers and names of the Executive Committee of the " Society for the Promotion of Manufactures," together with the Post Office address of each. Any communication addressed to either of them, or to the Society generally, will receive prompt attention:

ED. WILLIAMS, President...................... San Jose, Cal.
H. S. FOOTE, Secretary...................... San Jose, Cal.
F. FIELD, Treasurer........................ San Jose, Cal.

EXECUTIVE COMMITTEE.

JAMES A. CLAYTON............. .... San Jose, Cal.
WILSON HAYS.............................. San Jose, Cal.
JOSEPH ENRIGHT............................. San Jose, Cal.
G. McG. PATTERSON....................... San Jose, Cal.
ED. WILLIAMS .... San Jose, Cal.

THE SANTA CLARA VALLEY.

A Brief Statement in Regard to the County at Large.

ITS AGRICULTURAL AND HORTICULTURAL RESOURCES—EDU-
CATIONAL ADVANTAGES, ETC.

In the foregoing pages we have confined ourselves as nearly as practicable to the City of San Jose, it being the object of this work to present the advantages of that point as a manufacturing center. Our references to the county at large have been made incidentally as they seemed to be required for the purpose of explanation. We shall devote these few supplemental pages to the county, and endeavor to show, briefly, the

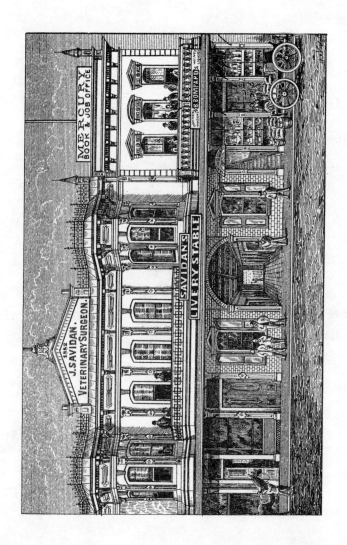

reason of our faith in the future importance of this community.

Our incomparable climate can not be adequately described. No one who has not experienced it can realize its invigorating influences. Our long season of health-inducing sunshine and ever blue sky, and our pure atmosphere, never too warm nor too cold for comfort, and possessing all the elements for vigorous animal and vegetable life, is unsurpassed anywhere on the globe. One peculiarity of our climate, which enables a person to do more work here than elsewhere, and with less fatigue, is the fact that he is always sure of a good rest at night. However warm the days may be, the nights are cool and exactly adapted to healthful sleep. No matter how much the laborer may be exhausted by his day's work, his energies are renewed at night and the morning finds him fresh for new duties.

We have alluded to our fruit interests and the bearing they have on our prosperity.

The magnitude of this interest can not be
fully understood by a stranger without some
further explanation.   In the earlier history
of the valley large quantities of fruit were
grown, but being without a market this
branch of business came into disrepute, and
orchards were either rooted up or suffered
to die from neglect.   The finding of an adequate market has given us an industry more
valuable than all the mines in this golden
State.   The art of preserving fruit has taken
this commodity out of the list of perishable
articles and has given us the whole world
for a customer.   The canned fruits of Santa
Clara County are sold in all the markets of
the globe, and the demand is far in excess
of the supply.

We have some varieties of fruit in common with other sections of the country, and
of course have competition as to them.
But we have varieties with which we beat
the world, and in which no competition is
possible.   For prunes, apricots, plums,

ARCHITECT.

L. Goodrich,

OFFICE, NO. 20 KNOX BLOCK,

San Jose, Cal.

G.P. GOODRICH, Arch't

Published by E. B. GOODRICH

Britton & Rey, Lith.

STATE NORMAL SCHOOL,
SAN JOSE, CAL.

peaches, grapes, etc., our climate and soil are such that no country on the globe can approach us in point of quantity and quality. We can raise more and better grapes to the acre than France, and the French prune raised in this valley is much richer and yields larger returns than in its native country. Here is essentially the home of the apricot, a luscious fruit with which the world was but little acquainted until introduced through the medium of our fruit packing establishments. As for peaches, plums, pears, etc., we can say nothing further than that they have excited wonder and admiration at all points where they have been shipped. But it is not so much our purpose to describe the varieties of fruits produced here as to show the profit of their production, and to this end a few figures will accomplish more than a hundred pages of description. Four years ago a San Francisco cannery made a contract with the owner of a ten acre orchard of apricot trees to take the fruit for five years, and pay him $5,000 per year for it. The purchaser is desirous of renewing the contract for another term, but the trees having grown much larger the owner demands, and will probably receive, a much higher price. S. D. Ayers got $450 during the past season for the crop on less than half an acre of young prune trees. There are numerous instances of like profit. These are larger returns than the average, but in an ordinarily fair season fruit growers expect to get from $250 to $300 per acre from their orchards. The cost of cultivation does not exceed $10 per acre. We will give some details: Good fruit land can be had at from $75 to $300 per acre, according to location. We will take the average, which is $200, and we have the following result:

Ten acres of land at $200	$2,000 00
Cultivation prior to planting	20 00
750 trees at 20c	150 00
Planting	60 00
Cultivation........................	20 00
	$2,250 00

This would be the entire outlay for the

first year. The cost of cultivation is made large enough to include the raising of a crop between the trees, if desired. For the second year we have the following expenses:

Pruning... $ 2 50
Plowing...   20 00
Cultivating.......................................   20 00
Sundries..   20 00
                                                    ————
                                                    $62 50

For the third, fourth and fifth years the expenses will be about the same as for the second year, which would give us the following result:

Cost of land and expenses 1st year.............. $2,250 00
Expenses 2d, 3d, 4th and 5th years..............   250 00
Add $15 00 per year for taxes 75 00
                                                    ————
                                                    $2,575 00

During these five years, if it is considered advisable, enough crop can be grown between the trees to pay the current expenses of the orchard. But outside of this, the yield from the fruit alone will average about as follows:

Third year, 75c per tree........................ $ 562 50
Fourth year, $1.50 per tree.....................   1,125 00
Fifth year, 2.50 per tree.......................   1,875 00
                                                    ————
                                                    $3,562 50

Making a profit for the five years of about a thousand dollars over and above cost of land, cultivation, and every other expense. At the end of the five years the orchard will be worth, in the market, anywhere from $500 to $1,200 per acre. After the fifth year there is practically no limit to the income. We saw ten year old apricot trees, last season, that would average $18 per tree, and one cherry orchard nine years old brought $11.50 per tree.

There has been but one doubt in the minds of our people as to the continuance of this almost fabulous income. It was feared by some that the immense area being planted to orchards would overtax the capacity for packing the fruit. In other words, that the supply would be so far in excess of the demand that adequate prices could not be obtained. This fear, however, has been proved to be groundless. In addition to the establishment of new canneries, the business of drying fruit has become quite

hird Ward School.

an industry. The competition between canneries and driers keeps up the price, and should this fail the fruit grower can dry or can his own crop with profit. If it should occur, from any unforseen circumstances, that the price of fruit should decline fifty per cent, or even more, it would still leave a magnificent profit to the orchardist.

What we have said here in regard to fruit growing is equally true of vine culture, whether the grapes be grown for raisins or wine. This industry has the advantage in the fact that the grape land can be had cheaper than fruit land. There is scarcely an acre of our hills on either side of the valley that is not adapted to this business, and these hill lands are held at considerably lower prices than the valley lands. Without going into the details of the expense and income of grape culture, we will give one firm's experience in this business, and it will stand for all. Five years ago Messrs. O'Banion and Kent purchased a tract of land and planted it to fruit. It cost them something over $4,000. A few weeks ago they sold their orchard for $60,000. In the meantime they had realized enough from their crops to pay the purchase price of their land, and a very handsome yearly income besides.

We have given these details, which are under, rather than over the mark, to prove the statement made in a preceding page, that five acres of land in this county would yield a handsome support for an ordinarily sized family. We have sufficient acreage of this kind of land in this county to support a quarter of a million families, and when we take into consideration the fact that the money for our produce all comes from abroad, and that its interchange among ourselves in the ordinary channels of trade will support in comfort an equal number of people, are we not justified in our faith in the future importance of this county?

A few years ago, James Lick, a wealthy

New York Exchange Hotel, Cor. First and St. John Sts.
WARKENTIN & BAYERSDORFER. Proprietors.

citizen of San Jose, gave his entire property, consisting of nearly five millions of dollars, to philanthropic institutions and works of public improvement in this State. The most important of these bequests was that of $750,000 for the establishment of an astronomical observatory on Mt. Hamilton, in this county, which was to be equipped with the most powerful telescope in the world. Mt. Hamilton is located in the range of mountains east of the valley, and is twenty miles distant from San Jose. It stands 4,400 feet above the level of the sea, in an atmosphere cloudless during the entire year. From its summit there is an unbroken horizon, while its latitude is favorable for the most important observations. The County of Santa Clara has constructed, at an expense of about $100,000, a magnificent road to the top of the mountain. This road is of easy grade, magnificently constructed, and furnishes a beautiful drive. The scenery along its route is unsurpassed for beauty and grandeur. The work on the observatory has been carried on as far as it is possible until the object glass for the great telescope is completed. The large lens is in course of construction by the famous house of Alvan Clark and Sons, of Cambridge, Massachusetts, and it is expected that it will be ready to place in position in about twelve months. The Trustees, who have the work in hand, are using every endeavor to carry out in spirit and in letter the terms of their trust, and with unlimited means at their disposal, there is every reason to believe that they will make the observatory what the donor intended, the greatest in the world. The buildings on the summit are completed as far as possible, and have been equipped with all the most improved instruments known to astronomical science. Pending the completion of the great glass, a 12-inch telescope has been mounted, and some important observations have been made. The mountain has already

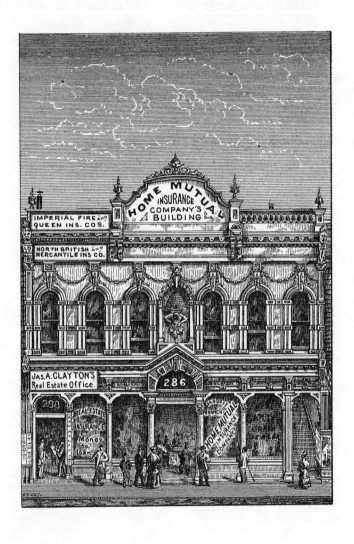

been visited by eminent astonomers from all parts of the world, and all unite in pronouncing the site most desirable and the conditions of the atmosphere the most perfect of any observatory within their knowledge. This was emphatically the opinion of the corps of astronomers sent out by the French Academy of Sciences to view the transit of Mercury. They spent several nights on Mt. Hamilton, and after testing the location in a most critical manner were enthusiastic in their commendations.

This party of scientists also bore witness to the importance of another of the resources of our county. In passing over the road to Mt. Hamilton they expressed their surprise that the thousands of acres of hills used for cattle ranges, with here and there a grain field, were not planted to vineyards. In France, they said, such land in such a location would be utilized for vines to its last acre. The soil and the climate is equal to that of the most famous vineyards of France.

And this brings us to the consideration of another matter. Thus far the western portion of the valley and the western hills have been known as the fruit section of this county. This has been the result of accident rather than any superiority of soil or climate which the western half of the county possesses over the eastern. There is a small section of country known as "The Willows," adjoining the city on the southwest, which, many years ago, was ascertained to be peculiarly adapted to the production of strawberries. From the culture of this fruit came successful experiments with blackberries and then larger fruits. The success of these ventures led to others, the area devoted to this industry gradually extending to the south, north and west of the willows until that portion of the county became known as the fruit belt. Another circumstance which has given the fruit "boom" to the western portion of the county is the fact that in the eastern portion the land has

MUSIC HALL BUILDING.

Hon. C. H. Maddox, Proprietor.

been held in large tracts which the owners were loth to divide. People who desired to make an orchard of ten or twenty acres did not wish to purchase a hundred acres of land for the purpose. This has, in a great measure, retarded the fruit business in that section. Experiments during the last four years have demonstrated that, in capacity for producing the best qualities of fruit and grapes, the eastern portion of the county is in no wise inferior to the western. The orchards of Messrs. Flickinger, Smith, Shaw, and others, in the neighborhood of Berryessa, conclusively demonstrate this. Some of the very best fruit and grape lands in the county lie to the east and south of San Jose, in the vicinity of the little village of Evergreen. This section has been hitherto devoted almost exclusively to grain growing, but scattering orchards, here and there, show its capabilities for the more profitable industry. Land in this particular section has hitherto been held in large farms, but these are now

being broken up, and in a few years this
portion of the county will realize its mani-
fest destiny. The fact that this section has
not been so swift to take hold of the fruit
business has led many superficial observers
to conclude that the land is not adapted to
that purpose. But those who have examined
the soil on the old Farnsworth place, now
the property of W. J. Cottle, and have seen
the fruit grown there, and elsewhere in the
vicinity, are convinced that this is a mistaken
idea. And it seems that this is becoming
the general opinion, for we notice that this
land is meeting with a ready sale for fruit
and vine purposes as rapidly as it is subdi-
vided into tracts of the required size.

The public highways of Santa Clara County
are not surpassed either in number or character by any county in the State. Our road
system is a matter to which every Board of
Supervisors, since the organization of the
county, has paid particular attention, and no
pains or expense has been spared to make it

Fourth Ward School.

B. J. RHODES & CO.,

LEADING DRUGGISTS,

No. 13 West Santa Clara Street,

SAN JOSE, CAL.

as perfect as possible. Broad avenues, systematically and scientifically graded and gravelled, penetrate every section, and there is not a farm, either in the valley or hills, which has not easy communication with a good substantial road. Some of these highways take rank with the famous avenues of the world. Among these is the Alameda, leading from San Jose to the town of Santa Clara, a distance of three miles, through double rows of gigantic willows over a century old. This beautiful avenue is famed in story and in song, and a detailed description in these pages is unnecessary. Another magnificent highway is the Santa Clara Avenue, leading from San Jose to the City Reservation in the eastern foothills, seven miles distant.

The consideration of our highways leads us to another point important to those looking for homes in the country. We refer to the facilities possessed by our farmers for reaching market with their produce. With three lines of railroad running to the north and two to the south, with stations at short intervals on each line, the farmer, wherever he may be located, has but a short distance to haul his produce.

We would not attempt, within the narrow limits of this book, published as it is for the information of manufacturers, to give a detailed description of all the advantages which our county offers to those seeking homes. There are some things, however, that are of first importance, and first among these is the question of education.   We point with pride to the schools and colleges of Santa Clara County.   Our common school system has had some of the best minds of the Nation at work in its arrangement, and this, backed by an unlimited supply of money, has given us a system second to none in the Union. From the primary school the grades run symmetrically up through the grammar schools, high schools, to the University of California, and all this is furnished to the pupil at public expense. It need cost the pupil nothing for instruction from the time he commences his alphabet until he graduates an A. B., or receives his diploma as a member of one of the learned professions. Our school buildings throughout the county are numerous and models of architecture. The course of study has received the approval of many of the best educators of the Nation, and our instructors are selected only after a most critical examination of their general learning and their ability to impart it. In addition to the educational facilities offered by our common school system, we have the Santa Clara College, a Catholic institution with a world-wide reputation, and the University of the Pacific, a Methodist institution with a curriculum and a corps of instructors equal to that of many of the most prominent eastern colleges. We have located at San Jose the State Normal School with an average attendance of over five hundred students from all portions of the State. We have private schools and academies, and schools of specialties, a Commercial College and a school of elocution and oratory. San Jose has a free public library containing some 10,000 volumes, with an assured income amply sufficient to keep its shelves supplied with the most important of new publications.

In the matter of religious privileges about all the orthodox denominations are represented, and all have comfortable houses of worship, some of the church buildings being magnificent specimens of architecture.

Our climate and natural advantages have attracted to our county people of culture and learning from all parts of the world. The result has been the organization of literary circles, art societies, musical societies, dramatic societies, and societies for studying specialties in all the different branches of science, literature and art. The doors of all these associations are open to every person of good moral character.

The list of fraternal societies is full. We

Hardware.

—

IRON, COAL AND STEEL

CHAMPION BARBED WIRE,

TOOLS OF ALL KINDS,

ETC., ETC.

—

HENRY B. ALVORD,

No. 27 First St., South,

SAN JOSE.

High School.

have the Masons, Odd Fellows, Workmen, Grand Army of the Republic, Patriotic Order of Sons of America, Good Templars, Champions of the Red Cross, Druids, Ancient Order of Hibernians, Knights of Pythias, Knights of Honor, Benevolent Societies of different nationalities, Granges, United Order of Red Men, Sons of Herman, Turn-Verein, and many others, including a Society of California Pioneers and The Native Sons of the Golden West.

We have an Agricultural Society, which is in a flourishing condition, annual exhibitions of stock, agricultural and mechanical products, which attract the attendance of large numbers of people from all portions of the State.

This society owns a beautiful tract of nearly one hundred acres on the line of the Alameda, and within a mile of the center of the city. These grounds are furnished with stables, stalls, corrals, and all other conveniences for the care and display of stock.

The mile track is conceded to be the best in the State, and has been the scene of some of the most famous racing events in the history of the country. The grounds are beautifully ornamented with trees and shrubbery, and during the past year a spacious pavilion has been erected for the exhibition of such articles as require to be under cover. The premiums offered amount to about $20,000 annually.

To sum everything up in a few words, we have, here in Santa Clara County, everything we want except factories to work up our raw material and to employ our surplus capital, and we hope and believe that when our advantages as a manufacturing center are fully realized we shall have all we want in that direction.

THE BANK OF SAN JOSE.
Established in 1866.

Capital, : : : : : $250,000
Reserve Fund, : : : : 100,000

T. ELLARD BEANS,.....President and Manager.
CLEMENT T. PARK...................Cashier.

Correspondents – Bank of California, San Francisco; Bank of British Columbia, San Francisco; Importers' and Traders' National Bank, New York; Oriental Bank Corporation, London.

TRANSACT A GENERAL BANKING BUSINESS, Buy and Sell Exchange, Bonds, Currency, County Scrip, and other Securities. Make Loans on Mortgages, Collaterals and Approved Notes; Receive Special and General Deposits.

JAMES R. LOWE,
ATTORNEY AT LAW,
NOTARY PUBLIC,
And COMMISSIONER OF DEEDS, for States and Territories,

18 and 19, Bank of San Jose Building, - - - SAN JOSE, CAL.
P O. BOX 552.

THOMAS H. CORDELL AND EDWARD HALSEY,
SEARCHERS OF RECORDS,
AND CONVEYANCERS,
Office, Room 7, Commercial Bank Building, SAN JOSE, CAL.

Refer to Members of the Bar, Santa Clara County.

THOMAS H. CORDELL, Notary Public.

Copies of Records and Abstracts of Title made at Lowest Rates. Prompt Personal Attention given to all Business.

W. A. PARKHURST,
Real Estate and Insurance Agent,
And NOTARY PUBLIC,
Office, Room No. 2, Knox Block, SAN JOSE, CALIFORNIA.

General Business Agency. Money Loaned, Searches Made, and Conveyancing Neatly Done. Real Estate Bought and Sold on Commission.
Houses Rented and Rents Collected.

☞ A Large List of Fine Farms. Also City and Suburban Property. Business left with me will receive Prompt Attention. Agent Commercial Fire Insurance Company, and Six of the Largest Fire Insurance Companies in the World. Combined Assets, $30,000,000.

E. H. GUPPY,

BOOKSELLER AND STATIONER

DEALER IN

SHEET MUSIC, SCHOOL FURNITURE, FANCY GOODS,

ETC., ETC.

361 FIRST STREET, SAN JOSE, CAL.

M. WILLARD,

IMPORTER AND JOBBER OF

Cigars and Tobaccos,

285 SANTA CLARA STREET,

Knox Block : : : : : : : San Jose.

The Trade Supplied at Short Notice.